Night Night

Learn about Healthy Sleep Habits with Sesame Street

Charlotte Reed

Lerner Publications ◆ Minneapolis

In this series, young readers will learn different ways they can take care of themselves! Come along as Elmo and his *Sesame Street* friends explore how healthy habits—like eating well and expressing your feelings—help you grow smarter, stronger, and kinder.

Sincerely,
the Editors at Sesame Workshop

Table of Contents

Healthy Sleeping

There are lots of ways you can take care of yourself. One important way to take care of yourself is by getting the same amount of sleep each night.

Everybody needs their sleep . . . even cute and adorable monsters like me!

Let's Get Ready for Bed!

Getting enough sleep gives us the energy to do things and helps us grow. When our bodies rest at night, we have energy during the day to play and learn!

Sleep also helps us take care of our minds. If we don't sleep well, we might feel grumpy or tired.

Yawn!
I feel sleepy
now.

Having a bedtime routine helps to let your mind and body know it's time to get ready for sleep. A bedtime routine is when you do the same things every night before bed.

When it's time to get ready for bed, you might take a bath or shower. Remember to always brush your teeth.

Brushing my teeth is the first thing I do when I get ready for bed!

13

There might be a special part of your bedtime routine you do each night. Maybe you read a book or sing a lullaby.

When it's time to get into your pajamas and get comfy and cozy under the blankets, you might look around the room and say good night to the objects you see.

I always say good
night to my doll Mimi!
Good night, Mimi!

When it's time to go to bed, there are lots of things you can do to help your mind and body feel sleepy.

You can try snuggling under the blanket, listening to soft music, or taking deep breaths!

Sleep is an important way to stay healthy. It's great to have a routine to help us get ready for bed.

Build a bedtime routine checklist. What do you do before bedtime? Make a list with your grown-up that you can check off every night. Here are some ideas:

- Change into pajamas.
- Brush your teeth.
- Go to the bathroom.
- Read a bedtime story.
- Snuggle with your stuffed animal.
- Sing a lullaby.
- Take deep breaths.

Glossary

bedtime: the time each night that you go to sleep

lullaby: a gentle song to be sung before bed

pajamas: what you wear to sleep at night

routine: things you do the same way every day or night

Read More

Monster Meditation: Getting Ready for Bed with Elmo. New York: Random House Children's Books, 2021.

Peters, Katie. *I Care for Myself.* Minneapolis: Lerner Publications, 2023.

Schuh, Mari. *Taking Care of Me: Healthy Habits with Sesame Street.* Minneapolis: Lerner Publications, 2021.

Photo Acknowledgments

Image credits: Maskot/Getty Images, p. 4; Elizaveta Starkova/Getty Images, p. 7; Choreograph/Getty Images, p. 8; Fuse/Getty Images, p. 11; somethingway/Getty Images, p. 12; PeopleImages/Getty Images, p. 15; SelectStock/Getty Images, p. 16; JGI/Tom Grill/Getty Images, p. 18; Tom Werner/Getty Images, p. 20. Design element: Dedraw Studio/Shutterstock.

Lerner Publications Company
An imprint of Lerner Publishing Group, Inc.
241 First Avenue North
Minneapolis, MN 55401 USA

For reading levels and more information, look up this title at www.lernerbooks.com.

Main body text set in Mikado. Typeface provided by HVD.

Designer: Laura Otto Rinne
Lerner team: Martha Kranes

Library of Congress Cataloging-in-Publication Data

Names: Reed, Charlotte, 1997– author.
Title: Night night : learn about healthy sleep habits with Sesame Street / Charlotte Reed.
Description: Minneapolis : Lerner Publications, [2025] | Series: Sesame Street self-care | Includes bibliographical references and index. | Audience: Ages 4–8 | Audience: Grades K–1 | Summary: "Young readers learn along with their friends from Sesame Street the importance of sleep and sleep routines. Then they discover how to make their own sleep routine"—Provided by publisher.
Identifiers: LCCN 2024012736 (print) | LCCN 2024012737 (ebook) | ISBN 9798765643723 (library binding) | ISBN 9798765662427 (paperback) | ISBN 9798765658031 (epub)
Subjects: LCSH: Sleep–Juvenile literature. | Self-care, Health–Juvenile literature.
Classification: LCC RA786 .R44 2025 (print) | LCC RA786 (ebook) | DDC 613.7/94–dc23/eng/20240516

LC record available at https://lccn.loc.gov/2024012736
LC ebook record available at https://lccn.loc.gov/2024012737

Manufactured in the United States of America
1-1010921-52413-7/10/2024